I0020417

Mastering YOLO:

Build an Automatic Number Plate Recognition System

OPENCV & PYTHON

Contents

Who should read this book?

This book is perfect for anyone who wants to learn how to apply deep learning, and specifically the YOLO model, to computer vision and real-time object detection. The book assumes the reader has some prior experience with Python and OpenCV but does not require professional proficiency in either. Whether you are a beginner or an experienced programmer, you will learn how to build an Automatic Number Plate Recognition System from scratch using the YOLO framework.

The step-by-step guide and clear explanations will help you gain a deep understanding of object detection concepts and the YOLO framework, and equip you with the skills to implement your object detection projects.

Roadmap

In this book, you will learn how to build an end-to-end automatic number plate recognition system using the state-of-the-art YOLO object detection algorithm. You will start by collecting and labeling your own dataset, then you will use it to train a custom YOLO model.

Next, you will learn how to use the trained model to detect number plates in images and real-time videos, and how to use OCR to recognize the text from the license plates.

Finally, you will build a simple web application using Streamlit and deploy the NPR system on it.

By the end of this book, you will have the skills to create your own number plate recognition system and apply it to real-world applications such as traffic monitoring, surveillance, and self-driving cars.

You can download the source code from this link (or from here: https://bit.ly/476fiJH)

About the Author

My name is Yacine Rouizi and as a self-taught Python programmer, I have a passion for creating content about machine learning, deep learning, and computer vision. My journey in programming began in 2019 and since then, I have been constantly learning and improving my skills. I share my knowledge and experiences essentially in the thepythoncode blog.

I hold a level 1 Master's degree in Physics, and I am originally from Algeria. I am thrilled to have the opportunity to share my passion for technology and programming with others. I believe that through clear explanations and practical examples, I can help make complex topics, such as deep learning and computer vision, accessible to everyone.

If you want to contact me, here is where you can find me:

Email: cinorouizi@gmail.com
Twitter: dontrepeatyourself
LinkedIn: Yacine Rouizi

1. What is Object Detection

Object detection is a computer vision technique for locating instances of objects in images or videos. It involves the identification of objects of interest within an image or video stream and the localization of these objects by drawing a bounding box around them. Object detection goes beyond image classification, which only identifies the presence of an object in an image but does not provide any location information.

Image Classification vs. Object Detection

Classification

Cat

Detection

Cat, Dog, Dog

V7 Labs

Image classification assigns a **label** to an entire image, while object detection **locates** and **identifies** individual objects within an image **and** assigns them a label. (image source)

Object detection algorithms typically leverage machine learning or deep learning to produce meaningful results. These algorithms are trained on large datasets of annotated images and use the learned representations to detect objects in new images.

Deep learning has revolutionized the field of object detection and has become the go-to method for solving this task. Convolutional Neural Networks (CNNs) are the most commonly used deep learning architecture for object detection. CNNs are designed to effectively handle high-dimensional image data and learn hierarchical representations that can capture the details in an image.

In real-world applications, object detection has a wide range of uses, including surveillance and security, self-driving cars, and augmented reality.

2. Advancements in Object Detection

Object detection has come a long way over the past 20 years, with significant advancements made in the field. Before the introduction of deep learning in 2012, object detection relied primarily on traditional machine learning techniques such as the Viola-Jones Detector, HOG Detector (Histogram of Oriented Gradients for Human Detection), deformable parts models, etc.

However, with the advent of deep learning, object detection has seen an unprecedented leap in performance. Today's deep learning-based approaches, such as YOLO, SSD, and R-CNN family of algorithms, make use of neural network architectures to accurately detect and classify objects.

Deep learning-based object detectors are generally divided into two main categories: one-stage and two-stage detectors.

One-stage detectors, such as YOLO, SSD, and RetinaNet, directly predict bounding boxes and class probabilities in a single pass. These algorithms are much faster than two-stage detectors but less accurate.

Two-stage detectors, such as RCNN, Faster R-CNN, and Mask R-CNN, use two networks: The first network, called a region proposal network (RPN), proposes regions where objects are likely to be present. The second network (a classifier) classifies the proposed regions into different classes of objects.

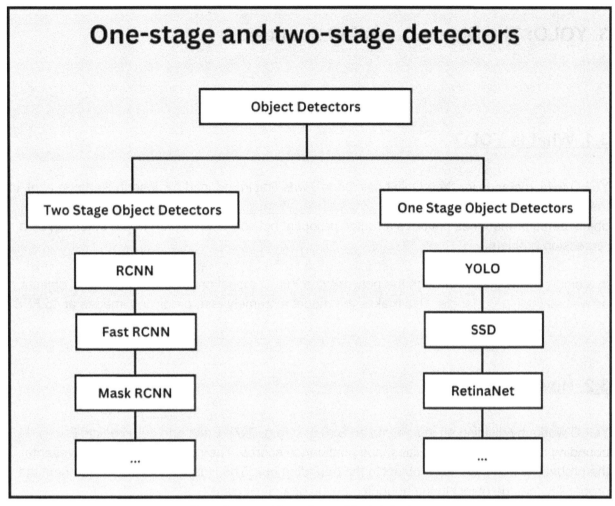

One-stage and two-stage object detectors

3. YOLO: The Object Detection Framework

3.1. What is YOLO

YOLO (which stands for "You Only Look Once") was first introduced by Joseph Redmon et al. in the 2016 paper You Only Look Once: Unified, Real-Time Object Detection. It is a single-stage object detector that does not have a region proposal network and instead treats detection as a regression problem.

In a single forward pass through the network, the YOLO model predicts the location of objects, as well as their class labels. This makes the model extremely fast, predicting images at 45 FPS on a GPU.

3.2. How YOLO works

YOLO works by dividing an image into an SxS grid (e.g. 7x7). Each grid cell predicts B (e.g. 2) bounding boxes, class probabilities, and confidence scores. The confidence score represents the probability that there is an object in the bounding box. The class probabilities represent the probability that the object in the bounding box is of a given class.

The final output of the YOLO model is an array of shape (S, S, Bx5 + C), where S is the number of grid cells, B is the number of bounding boxes per grid cell, and C is the number of classes. The last dimension contains the bounding box coordinates, confidence scores, and class probabilities.

So, for example, if S=7, B=2, and C=20, the output array will have a shape of (7, 7, 2x5 + 20). The 2x5 comes from the 2 bounding boxes per grid cell, each of which has 5 elements: x, y, w, h, and confidence score and 20 is the number of classes.

Since the model predicts bounding boxes for each grid cell, there will be multiple bounding boxes for the same object. To remove duplicate/overlapping bounding boxes, the model uses non-max suppression (NMS).

NMS selects the bounding box with the highest confidence score and removes any bounding boxes that overlap it by more than a certain threshold (e.g. 0.5) using the intersection over union (IoU) metric.

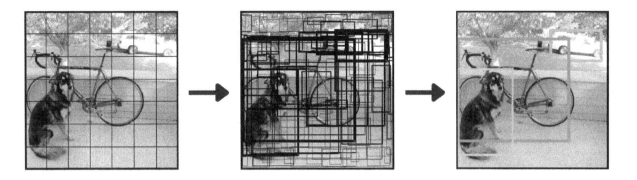

YOLO before and after non-max suppression (image source modified)

3.3. YOLO Architecture

The YOLO architecture is a convolutional neural network inspired by the GoogLeNet model. It is composed of 24 convolutional layers followed by 2 fully connected layers. The model takes in an input image of shape (448, 448, 3) and outputs a tensor of shape (7, 7, 30).

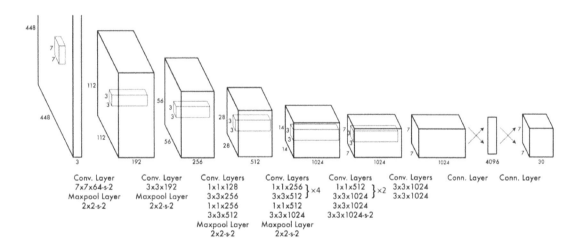

YOLO architecture (image source)

3.4. YOLO Versions

YOLO has gone through several iterations, with each iteration improving the speed and accuracy of the model.

I included in the table below the links to the papers for each version of YOLO. You can read the papers to learn more about the architecture and the improvements made in each version.

Version	Year	Paper
YOLOv1	2016	You Only Look Once: Unified, Real-Time Object Detection
YOLOv2	2017	YOLO9000: Better, Faster, Stronger
YOLOv3	2018	YOLOv3: An Incremental Improvement
YOLOv4	2020	YOLOv4: Optimal Speed and Accuracy of Object Detection
YOLOv5	2020	No paper
YOLOv6	2022	YOLOv6: A Single-Stage Object Detection Framework for Industrial Applications
YOLOv7	2022	YOLOv7: Trainable bag-of-freebies sets new state-of-the-art for real-time object detectors
YOLOv8	2023	No paper

These are the main versions of YOLO but there are also other versions that were developed by other researchers such as Scaled YOLOv4, YOLOX, PP-YOLO, etc.

Please note that after the release of YOLOv3, Joseph Redmon the author of YOLO stopped publishing papers for the YOLO object detection algorithm. So YOLOv4 and later versions were created by other researchers.

In this book, we will use the YOLOv8 model which is developed by Ultralytics. The YOLOv8 model can not only be used for object detection but also for other computer vision tasks such as image classification, instance segmentation, pose estimation, and object tracking. Check out the Ultralytics docs for more information.

Now that you have a general idea of what YOLO is and how it works, let's see how to use it to detect objects in images and videos.

4. Environment Setup

Before we start installing Miniconda, it is important to note that this environment setup is crucial for the successful completion of the project. Miniconda is a lightweight version of Anaconda that includes only conda (a package manager), Python, the packages they depend on, and a small number of other useful packages. This will make it easier to install and manage the packages and dependencies required for this project. Let's get started with the installation process.

Here, I will only be focusing on the installation and setup process on the Ubuntu operating system. The steps for other operating systems are quite similar.

4.1. Install Miniconda

Before installing any packages, we will first set up our environment by installing Miniconda and creating a virtual environment for our project. To install Miniconda, follow these steps:

1- Go to the official website and download the latest version of Miniconda for your operating system.

2- Once the download is complete, open the terminal and navigate to the directory where you downloaded the file. Then run the Miniconda installer:

```
$ bash Miniconda3-latest-Linux-x86_64.sh # for Linux
```

and follow the instructions on the screen.

3- Once the installation is complete, close the terminal and open a new one. Then run the following command to test if the installation was successful:

```
$ conda --version
conda 22.11.1
```

If you see the version number, then you have successfully installed Miniconda.

Now that we have installed Miniconda, we can create a virtual environment for our project. A virtual environment is an isolated environment where we can install packages and dependencies specific to our project, without interfering with other projects. To create a virtual environment, run the following command:

```
$ conda create --name yolov8
```

This will create a new virtual environment called **yolov8**. To activate the environment, you can run the following command:

```
$ conda activate yolov8
```

and to deactivate it, run:

```
$ conda deactivate
```

4.2. Install the Required Packages

Now that we have created our virtual environment, we can install the required packages and dependencies. The required packages for this project are:

- Label Studio (for labeling the dataset)
- The Ultralytics package
- EasyOCR (for performing OCR)
- Streamlit (for building our web application)
- OpenCV
- Scikit-learn
- YAML

We will start by installing the packages that we will need in the next chapter, which are OpenCV, Scikit-learn, and YAML. In later chapters, as we progress with the project, we will install the other required packages, such as Label Studio, Streamlit, and so on, when we need them. This way, we can keep our virtual environment organized and avoid installing packages that are not currently necessary for our project.

Okay, so to install the package needed for the next chapter, run the following command (make sure your conda environment is activated before installing the packages):

```
$ conda activate yolov8
$ pip install opencv-python scikit-learn pyyaml
```

4.3. Install CUDA and cuDNN for GPU support

As you may know, training deep learning models can be computationally intensive and time-consuming, especially when using large datasets. This is where GPUs come in handy. They are designed to perform complex and parallel computations, making the training process faster and more efficient.

CUDA is a parallel computing platform and API developed by NVIDIA, which enables GPU acceleration for general-purpose computing. In order to take advantage of GPU acceleration, we need to install CUDA on our system.

On the other hand, cuDNN is a library developed by NVIDIA for deep neural networks, it provides highly optimized and efficient implementations of common deep learning operations. Installing cuDNN will allow us to harness the power of our GPU for deep learning tasks and significantly speed up the training process.

Installing CUDA and cuDNN can be challenging but with Miniconda the process is streamlined and simplified. The separate environment created by Miniconda provides a controlled space for installing the necessary software for GPU support, including CUDA and cuDNN. This makes it easy to manage dependencies and avoid conflicts with other software on your system. So using Miniconda for GPU setup is a recommended best practice for a hassle-free installation experience.

Let's see now how to install CUDA and cuDNN using Miniconda. First, you need to install the NVIDIA GPU driver if you haven't already. You can find the latest version of the driver for your GPU on the NVIDIA website. Alternatively, you can open the **Software & Updates** app to install the driver.

Search for the "Software & Updates" application

Then, go to **Additional Drivers**, select the latest version of the driver for your GPU, and click **Apply Changes**.

List of NVIDIA drivers available

A third option is to use the command line to install the driver. To do that, run the following command:

```
# this is the latest version of the driver for my GPU
$ sudo apt install nvidia-driver-525
```

After the installation is complete, you need to reboot your system. Once your computer is back up, you can use the following command to check if the driver is installed correctly:

```
$ nvidia-smi
```

You should see something like this:

```
yacine@yacine:~$ nvidia-smi
Tue Feb  7 12:42:58 2023
+-----------------------------------------------------------------------------+
| NVIDIA-SMI 525.78.01    Driver Version: 525.78.01    CUDA Version: 12.0      |
|-------------------------------+----------------------+----------------------+
| GPU  Name        Persistence-M| Bus-Id        Disp.A | Volatile Uncorr. ECC |
| Fan  Temp  Perf  Pwr:Usage/Cap|         Memory-Usage | GPU-Util  Compute M. |
|                               |                      |               MIG M. |
|===============================+======================+======================|
|   0  NVIDIA GeForce ...   Off | 00000000:01:00.0  On |                  N/A |
| N/A   56C    P8     5W /  90W |     54MiB /  8192MiB |     16%      Default |
|                               |                      |                  N/A |
+-------------------------------+----------------------+----------------------+

+-----------------------------------------------------------------------------+
| Processes:                                                                  |
|  GPU   GI   CI        PID   Type   Process name                  GPU Memory |
|        ID   ID                                                   Usage      |
|=============================================================================|
|    0   N/A  N/A      2484      G   /usr/lib/xorg/Xorg                53MiB |
+-----------------------------------------------------------------------------+
```

Output of the command "*nvidia-smi*"

Next, you need to install the CUDA toolkit and cuDNN. This can be done by running the following command:

```
$ conda install -c conda-forge cudatoolkit=11.2 cudnn=8.1.0
```

Once the installation is complete, you can check if it was successful by running the following command:

```
$ conda list cud
# packages in environment at /home/yacine/miniconda3/envs/yolov8:
#
# Name                    Version                   Build  Channel
cudatoolkit               11.2.2                hbe64b41_10    conda-forge
cudnn                     8.1.0.77               h90431f1_0    conda-forge
```

If you see something similar to the output above, then the installation was successful.

To configure the system paths after installing CUDA Toolkit with conda, you need to set the environment variables to allow your system to recognize the CUDA installation. This can be done by adding the CUDA libraries to the dynamic library path, which the system uses to search for shared libraries. The following steps will guide you through the process:

Open a terminal window and enter the following command to create a new directory in the conda environment:

```
$ mkdir -p $CONDA_PREFIX/etc/conda/activate.d
```

Next, create a new shell script file named **env_vars.sh** by running the following command:

```
$ echo 'export LD_LIBRARY_PATH=$LD_LIBRARY_PATH:$CONDA_PREFIX/lib/' >
$CONDA_PREFIX/etc/conda/activate.d/env_vars.sh
```

This script sets the environment variable **LD_LIBRARY_PATH** to include the path to the CUDA libraries, which is located in the **$CONDA_PREFIX/lib/** directory.

So now, the system paths will be automatically configured when you activate this conda environment.

4.4. Project Structure

For this project, here is how we will organize our files and directories.

```
$ tree --filelimit 10
.
├── datasets
│   ├── car-number-plate
│   │   ├── classes.txt
```

```
|       |       ├── images    [279 entries]
|       |       ├── labels    [279 entries]
|       |       ├── labels.cache
|       |       ├── notes.json
|       |       └── videos
|       |           └── traffic.mp4
|       ├── images
|       |   ├── test   [59 entries]
|       |   ├── train  [195 entries]
|       |   └── valid  [25 entries]
|       └── labels
|           ├── test   [59 entries]
|           ├── train  [195 entries]
|           ├── valid  [25 entries]
├── detect_and_recognize.py
├── number-plate.yaml
├── preprocessing.py
├── runs
|   └── detect
|       └── train  [21 entries]
├── training.ipynb
├── web_app
|   ├── app.py
|   └── uploads
└── yolov8s.pt
```

Here is a brief description of each directory/file:

- **datasets**: This directory will contain all the data that we will use for training and testing our model. The **car-number-plate** folder will contain the images and annotations that we will use to train our custom YOLO model. The **images** and **labels** folders will be created programmatically by the **preprocessing.py** script. In this script, we will split the data into training, validation, and test sets. Finally, we have the **videos** folder which will contain a video that we can use to test our model in real-time.

- **detect_and_recognize.py**: Our main Python script that we will use for localizing license/number plates and performing OCR.

- **number-plate.yaml**: This is the configuration file that we will use to train our custom YOLO model.

- **preprocessing.py**: We split the dataset using this script. We will also use it to create our .yaml configuration file.

- **runs**: This directory will contain the results of our training. It will be created when we start training the YOLOv8 model.

- **training.ipynb**: As the name suggests, this is where we will be training our model.

- **web_app**: This directory will contain the code for our web application. It contains the **app.py** file which is the main script that we will use to build our web application.

- **yolov8s.pt**: This is the weights file that we will use to train our YOLO model. It will be downloaded automatically when we start training the YOLOv8 model.

With our project structure reviewed, let's get to work!

5. Data Preparation

Now that we have set up our environment, we can begin gathering the data that will be used to train the YOLO model.

There are many ways to collect the images to create the dataset. One option is to scrape images from the internet using a web scraping tool. This can be done by using a Python library such as Scrapy to automatically navigate and extract data from websites.

Another option is to use publicly available datasets, such as those available on robolow.com or kaggle.com. These datasets can be downloaded and used to train the model without any additional annotation work.

A third option is to manually search the internet for images using Google Images or any other search engine. Once you find the images, you can use a Google extension to download the images in bulk. Then you can use an annotation tool to manually draw bounding boxes around the objects in the images and save the annotations in a format that can be used for training.

It's important to note that the quality and quantity of the data will affect the performance of the model. The more data you have, and the more diverse it is, the better your model will perform. So, it's recommended to gather as much data as possible and make sure to have a diverse set of images to train your model on.

In our case, we will use the third option and manually search the internet for images of number plates so that you can see how to build a dataset from scratch and understand the process of annotation, which is a crucial step in object detection. This hands-on approach will help you develop a deeper understanding of the entire object detection process.

5.1. Gathering the Data

I found images from Flickr to be more relevant to our use case, so I will use this website to gather the images.

So go to flickr.com and search for the term "car number plate" and you will get a list of images.

Scroll down the page until you find a good variety of images (we want at least 200 images).

Flickr search results for the term *car number plate*

Now, we can use a Google Chrome extension to download the images in bulk. There are a lot of extensions that you can use to download images from the internet. One that I particularly like is called *Image Downloader*.

Image downloader Chrome extension

Go ahead, install the extension, click on it, then select all the images for the page and click on the "*Download*" button. You can even create a folder from the extension and save all the images in it.

Downloading images from Flickr using Image Downloader Chrome Extension

Once you have downloaded the images, it's important to go through them and eliminate any images that do not contain a number plate or are of poor quality. Open up the directory in which you saved the images and delete any images that are not relevant to our task or are of poor quality. We want to keep our dataset as clean as possible.

In the accompanying source code for this book, you will find these images (along with their annotations) in the **datasets/car-number-plate** directory. You can use them if you want to skip the steps outlined above.

If you take a look at the images from Flickr, you will notice that the majority of the images contain number plates that are close to the camera. While this may seem okay, it is important to remember that in real-world scenarios, number plates can be captured from a variety of distances.

A model that is only trained on images of number plates that are close to the camera may not be able to detect number plates that are farther away. This can lead to poor performance in real-world scenarios.

This may not be a huge problem for our case - remember that our end goal is to detect the number plates and then use Optical Character Recognition (OCR) to extract the text from them. Having a diverse dataset that includes number plates captured from different angles, distances, and lighting conditions is crucial, but detecting number plates that are too far away or too small, may not be useful as they might make it difficult for the OCR engine to recognize the text.

But don't worry, I have included additional images inside the **datasets/car-number-plate** directory which capture number plates from various distances and lighting conditions to improve the generalization of our YOLO model.

I wanted to take a moment to address this point before proceeding further in the book.

So now we are ready to start labeling our dataset. Let's find out how we can achieve this in the next section!

5.2. Labeling the Data

Now that we have gathered the images, we will be discussing the process of labeling the data.

Labeling the data is an essential step in the training process for object detection models such as YOLO. It involves manually drawing bounding boxes around the objects in the images and saving the annotations in a format that can be used for training.

There are many tools that you can use to label the data. One of the most popular tools is called LabelImg.

Unfortunately, LabelImg is no longer maintained and has become part of the Label Studio community. So, we will be using Label Studio instead.

Label Studio is a free and open-source data labeling tool that can be used to label images, text, hypertext, audio, video, and time-series data. It is a powerful tool that can be used to create custom annotation templates and export the annotations in a variety of formats.

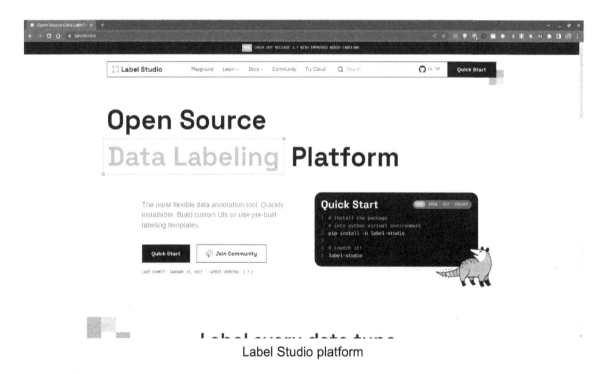
Label Studio platform

Label Studio is written in Django and can be installed using pip. So, let's go ahead and install it.

Make sure your conda environment is activated then run the following command to install Label Studio.

```
$ pip install label-studio
```

Once the installation is complete, you can start Label Studio by running the following command.

```
$ label-studio
=> Database and media directory: /home/yacine/.local/share/label-studio
=> Static URL is set to: /static/
=> Database and media directory: /home/yacine/.local/share/label-studio
=> Static URL is set to: /static/
Starting new HTTPS connection (1): pypi.org:443
https://pypi.org:443 "GET /pypi/label-studio/json HTTP/1.1" 200 54959
Performing system checks...

System check identified no issues (1 silenced).
January 24, 2023 - 11:31:01
Django version 3.2.16, using settings
'label_studio.core.settings.label_studio'
Starting development server at http://0.0.0.0:8080/
...
```

If you have already worked with the Django framework, the output of the command above will look familiar to you. It will start a local server on port 8080 and you can access it by going to **http://localhost:8080**.

Now, on the main page of Label Studio, you first need to create an account and then start a new project and import the images.

A new window will open and you can give a name for the project, then in the "**Data Import**" section, you can select the images that you want to label, and finally, you can choose a template for the labeling task from the "**Labeling Setup**" section.

In our case, we will use the "**Object Detection with Bounding Boxes**" template since our goal is to detect the number plates in the images and draw bounding boxes around them.

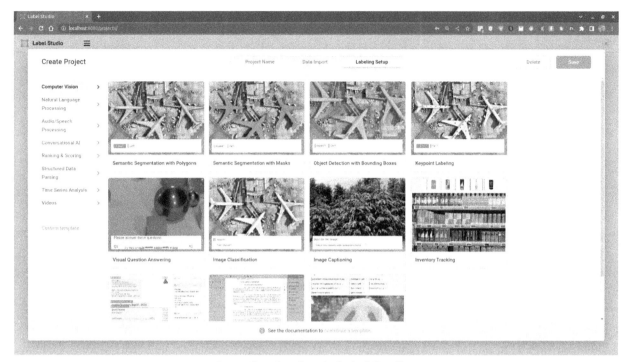

Importing the data in Label Studio

In the "***Object Detection with Bounding Boxes***" template, you can specify the label for the objects that you want to detect. In our case, we will use the label "Number Plate". Make sure to remove the default labels and add the label "Number Plate" to the list and then click on "Save".

Once you have configured the labeling task, you can click on the first image from the list to start labeling the images.

On the left side of the screen, you will see the image and on the right side, you will see the labeling interface. You can use the "Zoom" button to zoom in and out of the image and use the "Pan" button to move around the image.

To draw a bounding box around the number plate, you can click on the "Move" button, select the "Number Plate" label, and then click and drag to draw a bounding box around the number plate.

Draw a bounding box around the number plate in the image and then click on the "***Submit***" button to save the annotation. Repeat this process for all the images in the dataset.

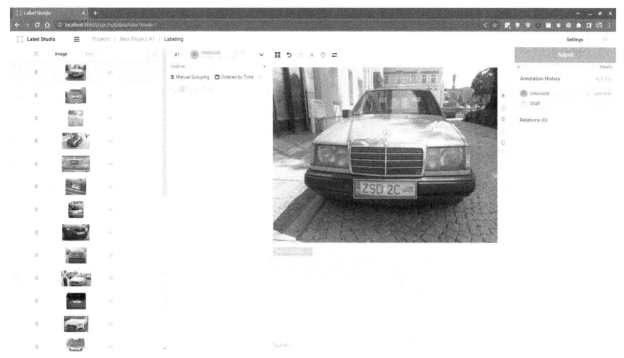

Labeling the images in Label Studio

Once you have labeled all the images, you can click on the "***Export***" button to export the annotations in a format that can be used for training.

When you click on the "***Export***" button, a new window will open and you can choose the format of the exported annotations. In our case, we will use the "YOLO" format since we will be using the YOLO object detection model.

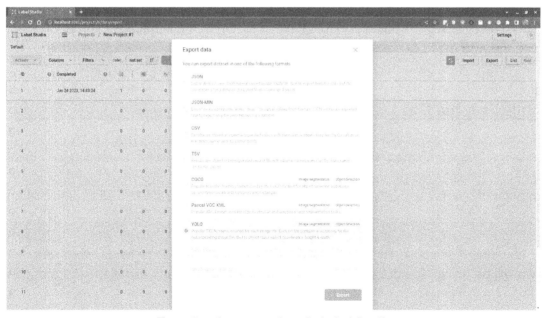

Exporting the annotations in Label Studio

Once you have downloaded the annotations, you can unzip the file and you will find two subdirectories. The "images" directory contains the images and the "labels" directory contains the corresponding annotations.

So far, we haven't talked about this, but it's crucial to understand that the YOLO model requires the data to be in a particular format, which includes a label file and an image file. The label file must contain the class label and the bounding box coordinates (**class_label, center_x, center_y, width, height**) per line. So, if there are 2 number plates in an image, the label file must contain 2 lines, with each line containing the bounding box coordinates and the class label of the number plate.

Here is an example of a label file:

```
0 0.496 0.6916 0.2863 0.10638
0 0.1496 0.916 0.8463 0.3651
```

So here we have 2 number plates in the image. The first line contains the class label (in our case, the class label will always be 0 because we are only detecting number plates) and the bounding box coordinates of the first number plate. The second line contains the class label and the bounding box coordinates of the second number plate.

As you can see, the bounding box coordinates are normalized. This means that the **center_x**, **center_y**, **width**, and **height** values are between 0 and 1. The **center_x** and **center_y** values represent the center of the bounding box, and the **width** and **height** values represent the width and height of the bounding box.

In our case, Label Studio takes care of this for us. It automatically generates the label file for us. So we don't have to worry about this. I just wanted to mention this because it's important to understand how the YOLO model works.

5.3. Splitting the Data

In this section, we will be discussing the process of splitting the data into training, validation, and testing sets. This is an important step in the training process as it allows us to evaluate the performance of our model during training and ensure that it generalizes well to new and unseen data.

We will be using the popular library scikit-learn to split our data into three different sets. In our case, we will be using 70% of the data for training, around 10% for validation, and around 20% for testing.

To split the data, we will write a Python script that will move the images and annotations to the corresponding directories. So, create a new file called **preprocessing.py** and add the following code to it.

```python
from sklearn.model_selection import train_test_split
import cv2
import os
import yaml


root_dir = "datasets/car-number-plate/"
valid_formats = [".jpg", ".jpeg", ".png", ".txt"]

def file_paths(root, valid_formats):
    "get the full path to each image/label in the dataset"
    file_paths = []

    # loop over the directory tree
    for dirpath, dirnames, filenames in os.walk(root):
```

The first thing that we do in the script is to import the required libraries. We will be using the scikit-learn library to split the data into training, validation, and testing sets.

Next, we define the root directory of the dataset and a list of valid file extensions for images and labels. Then, we define a function called **file_paths** that will return the full path to each image/label in the dataset. The function takes two arguments, the root directory of the dataset and the list of valid file extensions.

We are using the **os.walk** method to traverse the directory tree and extract the filenames of all the files in the dataset.

Now, we will loop over the filenames in the directory and add the path to the file to the **file_paths** list.

```python
        # loop over the filenames in the current directory
        for filename in filenames:
            # extract the file extension from the filename
            extension = os.path.splitext(filename)[1].lower()

            # if the filename has a valid extension we build the full
            # path to the file and append it to our list
            if extension in valid_formats:
```

```
            file_path = os.path.join(dirpath, filename)
            file_paths.append(file_path)

    return file_paths
```

Here, we are looping over the filenames in the current directory and extracting the file extension from the filename. We then check if the filename has a valid extension (an image or a txt file) and if it is, we build the full path to the file and append it to our list.

Finally, we return the list of file paths.

Let's test out our function:

```
>>> from preprocessing import file_paths
>>> root_dir = "datasets/car-number-plate/"
>>> valid_formats = [".jpg", ".jpeg", ".png", ".txt"]
>>> image_paths = file_paths(root_dir + "images", valid_formats[:3])
>>> image_paths
['datasets/car-number-plate/images/3e95e298-214.jpeg',
 'datasets/car-number-plate/images/f2f0b6f0-77.jpeg', ...]
>>> label_paths = file_paths(root_dir + "labels", valid_formats[-1])
>>> label_paths
['datasets/car-number-plate/labels/e87016c2-37.txt',
 'datasets/car-number-plate/labels/f2f0b6f0-77.txt', ...]
```

Notice that we are using the first three elements of the **valid_formats** list to get the authorized formats for the images and the last element to get the authorized format for the annotations.

As you can see, the **file_paths** function returns the list of paths to the images/labels in the dataset. So now, we can use the **file_paths** function to get the list of paths to the images/annotations in the dataset.

```
image_paths = file_paths(root_dir + "images", valid_formats[:3])
label_paths = file_paths(root_dir + "labels", valid_formats[-1])

# split the data into training, validation and testing sets
X_train, X_val_test, y_train, y_val_test = train_test_split(image_paths,
label_paths, test_size=0.3, random_state=42)
X_val, X_test, y_val, y_test = train_test_split(X_val_test, y_val_test,
test_size=0.7, random_state=42)
```

We split the data into training, validation, and testing sets using the **train_test_split** function. The **random_state** parameter is used to ensure that the same split is obtained every time the script is run.

Let's now create another function that will take the list of paths to the images/annotations and write them to the corresponding directories.

```python
def write_to_file(images_path, labels_path, X):

    # Create the directories if they don't exist
    os.makedirs(images_path, exist_ok=True)
    os.makedirs(labels_path, exist_ok=True)

    # loop over the image paths
    for img_path in X:
        # Get the image name and extension
        img_name = img_path.split("/")[-1].split(".")[0]
        img_ext = img_path.split("/")[-1].split(".")[-1]
```

The function takes 3 parameters:

- **images_path**: the path to the images directory where the images will be written to
- **labels_path**: the path to the annotations directory where the annotations will be written to
- **X**: the list of paths to the images. We only need to give the function the list of paths to the images since the labels have the same name as the images.

The function first creates the directories if they don't exist and then loops over the image paths. For each image path, we get the image name and its extension.

Now that we have the path to each image, its name, and its extension, we can read the image and write it and its corresponding annotation to the corresponding directories.

```python
    # read the image
    image = cv2.imread(img_path)
    # save the image to the images directory
    cv2.imwrite(f"{images_path}/{img_name}.{img_ext}", image)

    # open the label file and write its contents to the new label file
    f = open(f"{labels_path}/{img_name}.txt", "w")
    label_file = open(f"{root_dir}/labels/{img_name}.txt", "r")
    f.write(label_file.read())
```

```
        f.close()
        label_file.close()
```

So here we are reading the image and then we save it to the images directory. Next, we open the label file and write its contents to the new label file. Finally, we close the files.

We have finished writing our function. Now we can use it to write the images/annotations to the corresponding directories:

```
write_to_file("datasets/images/train", "datasets/labels/train", X_train)
write_to_file("datasets/images/valid", "datasets/labels/valid", X_val)
write_to_file("datasets/images/test", "datasets/labels/test", X_test)
```

Let's open the terminal and run it. Make sure you are in the project directory where the **preprocessing.py** file is located.

```
$ python preprocessing.py
```

After running the script, you should see two new directories in the **datasets** directory: **images** and **labels**. Inside each of these directories, you should see three new directories: **train**, **valid**, and **test**.

```
$ tree --filelimit 10 datasets/
datasets/
├── car-number-plate
│   ├── classes.txt
│   ├── images  [279 entries]
│   ├── labels  [279 entries]
│   ├── labels.cache
│   ├── notes.json
│   └── videos
│       └── traffic.mp4
├── images
│   ├── test  [59 entries]
│   ├── train  [195 entries]
│   └── valid  [25 entries]
└── labels
    ├── test  [59 entries]
    ├── train  [195 entries]
    └── valid  [25 entries]
```

5.4. Creating the YAML File

Okay, so now we have our dataset ready for training. The last thing we need to do is to create the YAML configuration file that will be used to train the model.

It will contain information about our dataset (i.e. the path to the train/valid/test directories and the classes in the dataset). Inside the **preprocessing.py** script insert the following code:

```python
# Create a dictionary with the paths to the train, valid, and test sets
data = {
    "path": "../datasets", # dataset root dir (you can also use the full
path to the `datasets` folder)
    "train": "images/train", # train images (relative to 'path')
    "val": "images/valid", # val images (relative to 'path')
    "test": "images/test", # test images (optional)

    # Classes
    "names":["number plate"]
}

# write the dictionary to a YAML file
with open("number-plate.yaml", "w") as f:
    yaml.dump(data, f)
```

Now, we need to run the script to create the YAML file. Make sure to comment out the code that creates the train/valid/test directories. Alternatively, you can delete the directories before running the script again. After running the script you should see a new file called *number-plate.yaml* in the project directory.

```
$ python preprocessing.py
$ tree -L 1

├── datasets/
├── number-plate.yaml # (new file)
├── preprocessing.py
```

Congratulations! You have successfully created the dataset and the YAML file. In the next part, we will start training the model.

6. Training the YOLO Model

Now that we have split our data into training, validation, and testing sets, and created our YAML file to define the configuration settings for our model, it's time to move on to the interesting step in our process: training the YOLO model.

During this process, the model will learn to detect the number plates from our dataset, and it will be able to generalize to new, unseen images.

The training process is vital for the performance of the model, therefore, it is essential to ensure that all details are properly set up and double-check everything before starting the training. This includes checking that the dataset is labeled correctly, the data is in the correct format, and there are no corrupt files.

We will be using the YOLOv8 implementation, which is a state-of-the-art object detection model that is known for its high performance and speed. So, let's begin this exciting step and start training our YOLO model!

6.1. Choose a Model

There are 5 pre-trained models available: yolov8n, yolov8s, yolov8m, yolov8l, and yolov8x.

Model	size (pixels)	mAP^{val} 50-95	Speed CPU ONNX (ms)	Speed A100 TensorRT (ms)	params (M)	FLOPs (B)
YOLOv8n	640	37.3	80.4	0.99	3.2	8.7
YOLOv8s	640	44.9	128.4	1.20	11.2	28.6
YOLOv8m	640	50.2	234.7	1.83	25.9	78.9
YOLOv8l	640	52.9	375.2	2.39	43.7	165.2
YOLOv8x	640	53.9	479.1	3.53	68.2	257.8

source

Each model is designed to provide a different balance between accuracy and speed, and the choice of model will depend on the specific requirements of your application. yolov8n is the smallest and fastest, while yolov8x is the largest and slowest.

We will be using the yolov8s model for this project. It is a good practice to start with the smallest model and see if the results are satisfactory. If not, you can try a larger model.

6.2. Start Training

Before starting training the model, we need to install the Ultralytics package. Create a new file called **training.ipynb** and run the following command:

```
!pip install ultralytics
```

After the installation is complete, we can start training the model by using the YOLO command line interface (CLI):

```
!yolo task=detect mode=train model=yolov8s.pt data=number-plate.yaml epochs=50
```

The **yolo** command takes several arguments. In the command above, we are passing the path to our YAML file and specifying that we want to use the pre-trained weights for the yolov8s model. We are also using the **--epochs** argument to specify that we want to train the model for 50 epochs (I found that using 50 epochs for training gives quite a good result).

It's also possible to pass additional arguments such as the batch size, the image size, the optimizer, etc. These arguments can be found on the Configuration page and can be used to fine-tune the training process.

Below you can see the output of the training. I truncated the output for brevity.

It shows some useful information such as the hyperparameters used, the GPU (in my case, it's an NVIDIA GeForce RTX 2070), The PyTorch version (1.10), etc.

```
Downloading https://github.com/ultralytics/assets/releases/download/v0.0.0/yolov8s.pt to
'yolov8s.pt'...
100%|████████████████████████████████████| 21.5M/21.5M [01:50<00:00, 205kB/s]
Ultralytics YOLOv8.0.196 🚀 Python-3.9.15 torch-1.10.2+cu102 CUDA:0 (NVIDIA GeForce RTX 2070
with Max-Q Design, 7974MiB)
engine/trainer: task=detect, mode=train, model=yolov8s.pt, data=number-plate.yaml,
epochs=50, …
Overriding model.yaml nc=80 with nc=1


...
```

```
Logging results to runs/detect/train
Starting training for 50 epochs...


        Epoch    GPU_mem   box_loss   cls_loss   dfl_loss  Instances       Size
         1/50     6.38G      1.351      4.346      1.263          7       640: 1
                Class     Images  Instances      Box(P          R      mAP50   m
                  all         25         58      0.105      0.448     0.0869     0.0548



         . . .


        Epoch    GPU_mem   box_loss   cls_loss   dfl_loss  Instances       Size
        50/50     6.48G      0.676     0.3901     0.8913          3       640: 1
                Class     Images  Instances      Box(P          R      mAP50   m
                  all         25         58      0.891      0.828      0.862      0.594

50 epochs completed in 0.125 hours.
Optimizer stripped from runs/detect/train/weights/last.pt, 22.5MB
Optimizer stripped from runs/detect/train/weights/best.pt, 22.5MB

Validating runs/detect/train/weights/best.pt...
Ultralytics YOLOv8.0.196 🚀 Python-3.9.15 torch-1.10.2+cu102 CUDA:0 (NVIDIA GeForce RTX 2070
with Max-Q Design, 7974MiB)
Model summary (fused): 168 layers, 11125971 parameters, 0 gradients, 28.4 GFLOPs
                Class     Images  Instances      Box(P          R      mAP50   m
                  all         25         58      0.903      0.806      0.867      0.604
Speed: 0.3ms preprocess, 4.3ms inference, 0.0ms loss, 0.5ms postprocess per image
Results saved to runs/detect/train
```

Well done! You have successfully trained the YOLOv8 model on a custom dataset.

The training took about 7.5 minutes to complete on my RTX 2070 GPU. The training process is quite fast since our dataset is not very big.

The YOLOv8 model outputs the training results to the **runs/detect/train** directory and each time you rerun the script, a new incrementing directory will be created (e.g. **train**, **train1**, **train2**, etc.)

The training results include the model weights (**best.pt** and **last.pt** inside the **weights** directory), various plots, and some images showing the results of the model. The **best.pt** file contains the weights of the model that performed the best on the validation set, so we will use this file for inference in the next section.

7. Detecting Number Plates with the Trained Model

In this section, we will use the weights obtained from training the YOLOv8 model to perform inference on new images. We will use the trained model to detect number plates in images and save their bounding boxes in a list so that we can use them later for Optical Character Recognition (OCR) to extract the text from the number plates.

7.1. Number Plate Detection in Images

We will write the code for detecting number plates in a function inside a script that we will call **detect_and_recognize.py**. We will do the same for the OCR part in the next part. Doing so will make it easier for us to reuse the code in our web application. So let's get our hands dirty and write some code:

```python
from ultralytics import YOLO
from easyocr import Reader
import time
import torch
import cv2
import os
import csv


CONFIDENCE_THRESHOLD = 0.4
COLOR = (0, 255, 0)

def detect_number_plates(image, model, display=False):
    start = time.time()
    # pass the image through the model and get the detections
    detections = model.predict(image)[0].boxes.data
```

The first thing we are doing in our script is importing the required libraries. As you can see in the code above, we are importing the **YOLO** class from the ultralytics library. We are also importing the **Reader** class from the **easyocr** library. We will use this class to perform OCR on the detected number plates.

EasyOCR is a Python library that makes it easy to perform OCR on images. It supports 80+ languages and is pip installable. You can install it with the following command:

```
$ pip install easyocr
```

We are also importing the **time** library to measure the time it takes to perform inference on images and real-time video streams. We will also use the **time** library to compute the FPS (Frames Per Second) of videos.

Next, we are loading the **torch** library and the **cv2** library to read the image and draw the bounding boxes on it. The **os** library will be used later on to extract the file's name and extension and the **csv** library will be used to write the bounding boxes to a CSV file.

The **detect_number_plates** function is our function for detecting number plates in images and videos. It takes two required arguments and one optional argument: the image and the model. The optional argument is a boolean that determines whether or not to display the image.

Inside the function, we are starting the timer and passing the image through the model. The model returns a tensor with the bounding boxes, their respective confidence scores, and the class labels (since we have only 1 class, the label will always be 0). We will use this tensor to draw the bounding boxes on the image.

Here is an example of the output of the model:

```
tensor([[ 89.81568, 156.58519, 137.54558, 182.16048,   0.85095,
0.00000]], device='cuda:0')
```

The first four elements of this tensor represent the bounding box coordinates (**xmin**, **ymin**, **xmax**, **ymax**). The fifth element is the confidence score and the last element is the class label.

Now that we have our detections, let's loop over them and keep only the ones with a confidence score above the threshold we set earlier.

```python
# check to see if the detections tensor is not empty
if detections.shape != torch.Size([0, 6]):

    # initialize the list of bounding boxes and confidences
    boxes = []
    confidences = []

    # loop over the detections
    for detection in detections:
        # extract the confidence (i.e., probability) associated
        # with the prediction
```

```
        confidence = detection[4]

        # filter out weak detections by ensuring the confidence
        # is greater than the minimum confidence
        if float(confidence) < CONFIDENCE_THRESHOLD:
            continue

        # if the confidence is greater than the minimum confidence, add
        # the bounding box and the confidence to their respective lists
        boxes.append(detection[:4])
        confidences.append(detection[4])

    print(f"{len(boxes)} Number plate(s) have been detected.")
# if there are no detections, show a custom message
else:
    print("No number plates have been detected.")
    return []
```

In the case where our model does not detect any number plates, it will return a tensor with a shape of (0, 6). So we check for this condition and if it is true, we show a custom message and return an empty list.

If the model detects number plates (**detections.shape != torch.Size([0, 6])**), we initialize two lists: one for the bounding boxes and one for the confidence scores.

Then we loop over the detections and get the confidence score for the current detection. If the confidence score is less than the threshold we set earlier, we will skip the current detection and move on to the next one using the **continue** statement. Otherwise, we will add the bounding box and the confidence score to their respective lists.

Let's continue writing our function. The next step is to loop over the list of bounding boxes to draw them on the image and return the list of bounding boxes.

```
if detections.shape != torch.Size([0, 6]):

    # ...

    print(f"{len(boxes)} Number plate(s) have been detected.")
    # initialize a list to store the bounding boxes of the
    # number plates and later the text detected from them
    number_plate_list= []
```

```python
        # loop over the bounding boxes
        for i in range(len(boxes)):
            # extract the bounding box coordinates
            xmin, ymin, xmax, ymax = int(boxes[i][0]), int(boxes[i][1]),\
                                     int(boxes[i][2]), int(boxes[i][3])
            # append the bounding box of the number plate
            number_plate_list.append([[xmin, ymin, xmax, ymax]])

            # draw the bounding box and the label on the image
            cv2.rectangle(image, (xmin, ymin), (xmax, ymax), COLOR, 2)
            text = "Number Plate: {:.2f}%".format(confidences[i] * 100)
            cv2.putText(image, text, (xmin, ymin - 5),
                        cv2.FONT_HERSHEY_SIMPLEX, 0.5, COLOR, 2)

            if display:
                # crop the detected number plate region
                number_plate = image[ymin:ymax, xmin:xmax]
                # display the number plate
                cv2.imshow(f"Number plate {i}", number_plate)

        end = time.time()
        # show the time it took to detect the number plates
        print(f"Time to detect the number plates: {(end - start) *
1000:.0f} milliseconds")
        # return the list containing the bounding
        # boxes of the number plates
        return number_plate_list
```

So here inside the if statement, we are adding the above code after getting the bounding boxes and the confidence scores.

First, we initialize a list to store the bounding boxes of the number plates along with the text associated with them (we will add the text later with OCR).

Next, we loop over the list of bounding boxes and extract the coordinates of the current bounding box. We store the bounding box in the **number_plate_list** list and draw a rectangle and the confidence score on the image.

If the **display** flag is set to **True**, we crop the detected number plate region and display it. Finally, we print the time it took to detect the number plates and return the list containing the bounding boxes.

All right! We are done with the **detect_number_plates** function. Let's write some code to test it on images.

```
# ...

def detect_number_plates(image, model, display=False):
    # ...

# if this script is executed directly, run the following code
if __name__ == "__main__":

    # load the model from the local directory
    model = YOLO("runs/detect/train/weights/best.pt")
    # initialize the EasyOCR reader
    reader = Reader(['en'], gpu=True)

    # path to an image or a video file
    file_path = "datasets/images/test/0fc216ca-131.jpg"
    # Extract the file name and the file extension from the file path
    _, file_extension = os.path.splitext(file_path)

    # Check the file extension
    if file_extension in ['.jpg', '.jpeg', '.png']:
        print("Processing the image...")
```

The **if __name__ == "__main__":** block is used to specify that the code within it will only be executed if the script is run directly. The code within this block will not be executed if we import the script as a module.

This is necessary since we will be importing the **detect_number_plates** function in our web application. We don't want the code within the **if __name__ == "__main__":** block to be executed when we import the script as a module.

So inside this block, we are loading the pre-trained YOLOv8s model from the local directory using the YOLO class. We are also initializing the EasyOCR reader which will be used to extract the text from the detected number plates later. Next, we are getting the path to an image or a video file and extract the file name and the file extension from the file path. Make sure to download the source code to get the images and video files.

If the file is an image, we will process it using the **detect_number_plates** function

```
        image = cv2.imread(file_path)
```

```
            number_plate_list = detect_number_plates(image, model,
                                                      display=True)
            cv2.imshow('Image', image)
            cv2.waitKey(0)
```

In the code above we are simply reading the image using OpenCV and passing it to the **detect_number_plates** function. We are also setting the **display** flag to **True** so that the detected number plates will be displayed.

Let's now test our script:

```
$ python detect_and_recognize.py
```

If you are getting this error after running the script:

```
Traceback (most recent call last):
  File "detect_and_recognize.py", line 151, in <module>
    number_plate_list = detect_number_plates(image, model,
  File "detect_and_recognize.py", line 63, in detect_number_plates
    cv2.imshow(f"Number plate {i}", number_plate)
  File "/content/yolov5/utils/general.py", line 1130, in imshow
    imshow_(path.encode('unicode_escape').decode(), im)
cv2.error: OpenCV(4.5.4)
/tmp/pip-req-build-khv2fx3p/opencv/modules/highgui/src/window.cpp:1274:
error: (-2:Unspecified error) The function is not implemented. Rebuild the
library with Windows, GTK+ 2.x or Cocoa support. If you are on Ubuntu or
Debian, install libgtk2.0-dev and pkg-config, then re-run cmake or
configure script in function 'cvShowImage'
```

Then you need to reinstall OpenCV. The error says that the function **cv2.imshow** is not implemented, meaning that the OpenCV library you are using doesn't have support for GUI functionality like displaying images in a window. This is caused by EasyOCR. EasyOCR installs a version of OpenCV that doesn't have GUI support. To fix this, we need to reinstall OpenCV.

```
$ pip uninstall opencv-python-headless
$ pip uninstall opencv-python
$ pip install opencv-python
```

After running the above commands, you should be able to run the script without any issues.

Here is the output of the script.

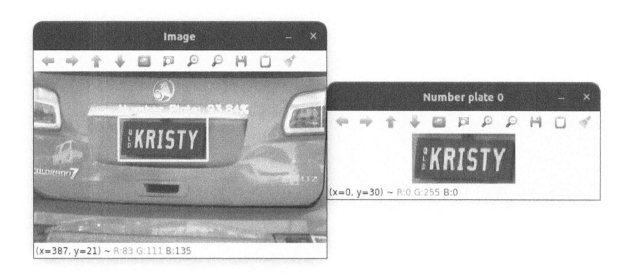

Number plate detection on an image

Take a look at your terminal. You should see something like this:

```
Processing the image...

0: 384x640 1 number plate, 8.7ms
Speed: 2.1ms preprocess, 8.7ms inference, 1.1ms postprocess per image at
shape (1, 3, 384, 640)
1 Number plate(s) have been detected.
Time to detect the number plates: 249 milliseconds
```

Our model has successfully detected the number plate on the image with a confidence score of 93.84%. That's pretty good! In the terminal, you can see that it took 249 milliseconds to detect the number plate using the GPU.

Let's test with another image that contains multiple number plates (**7cfaeef1-204.jpeg**):

Number plate detection on an image with multiple number plates

Okay, so here we have three number plates on the image but our model has only detected two of them. The third one is not detected because it is too small, this is quite normal.

However, we can improve the accuracy of our model by fine-tuning its parameters and training it with more images. But our goal here is to build a working prototype that we can use as a starting point for building our own number plate recognition projects. So we will not be fine-tuning the model.

7.2. Number Plate Detection in Videos

Now that we have seen how to detect number plates in images, let's see how to detect number plates in videos. We will be using our **detect_number_plates** function to detect number plates in videos. The only difference is that we will be using OpenCV to read the video frame by frame and pass each frame to the **detect_number_plates** function.

So inside the **if __name__ == "__main__":** block, let's add the following code:

```python
if __name__ == "__main__":

    # ...

    if file_extension in ['.jpg', '.jpeg', '.png']:
```

```
        # ...
    elif file_extension in ['.mp4', '.mkv', '.avi', '.wmv', '.mov']:
        print("Processing the video...")

        video_cap = cv2.VideoCapture(file_path)

        # grab the width and the height of the video stream
        frame_width = int(video_cap.get(cv2.CAP_PROP_FRAME_WIDTH))
        frame_height = int(video_cap.get(cv2.CAP_PROP_FRAME_HEIGHT))
        fps = int(video_cap.get(cv2.CAP_PROP_FPS))
        # initialize the FourCC and a video writer object
        fourcc = cv2.VideoWriter_fourcc(*"mp4v")
        writer = cv2.VideoWriter("output.mp4", fourcc, fps,
                                    (frame_width, frame_height))
```

When we are processing a video, we will be using OpenCV to read the video frame by frame. We initialize the video capture object using the **cv2.VideoCapture** class.

Before initializing the video writer object, we get the width, height, and frame rate of the video. The video writer object will be used to write the output video with the detected number plates.

Let's continue our video processing code; now we will be looping over the video frames:

```
        # loop over the frames
        while True:
            # starter time to computer the fps
            start = time.time()
            success, frame = video_cap.read()

            # if there is no more frame to show, break the loop
            if not success:
                print("There are no more frames to process."
                    " Exiting the script...")
                break

            number_plate_list = detect_number_plates(frame, model)
```

In the code snippet above, we are looping over the video frames using the **while True:** loop. Inside the loop, we grab the next frame from the video using the **video_cap.read()** function.

The function returns two elements: a boolean value *success* and the frame itself. If the **success** variable is **False**, it means that there is no more frame to read. In this case, we break the loop.

If the **success** variable is **True**, this indicates that we have successfully read the next frame from the video, so we can pass it to the **detect_number_plates** function.

The last step is to display and write the output video with the detected number plates:

```python
        # end time to compute the fps
        end = time.time()
        # calculate the frame per second and draw it on the frame
        fps = f"FPS: {1 / (end - start):.2f}"
        cv2.putText(frame, fps, (50, 50),
                    cv2.FONT_HERSHEY_SIMPLEX, 2, (0, 0, 255), 8)

        # show the output frame
        cv2.imshow("Output", frame)
        # write the frame to disk
        writer.write(frame)
        # if the 'q' key is pressed, break the loop
        if cv2.waitKey(10) == ord("q"):
            break

    # release the video capture, video writer, and close all windows
    video_cap.release()
    writer.release()
    cv2.destroyAllWindows()
```

We are calculating the frame per second (fps) and drawing it on the frame. We are also displaying the output frame and writing it to disk.

Finally, we are releasing the video capture, video writer, and closing all windows.

Let's now test our script. We will be using the **traffic.mp4** video, so make sure to change the **file_path** variable to the path of the video before running the script.

```python
# change this line inside detect_and_recognize.py
file_path = "datasets/car-number-plate/videos/traffic.mp4"

# run the script in the terminal
$ python detect_and_recognize.py
```

8. Recognizing Number Plates Using OCR

In this part, we will build on the work we did in the previous part and learn how to recognize the text in the detected number plates. We will use Optical Character Recognition (OCR) technology to extract the text from the bounding boxes obtained in the detection step.

OCR is the process of converting images or scanned documents into machine-readable text. By combining the number plate detection and OCR capabilities, we will have a complete system for automatically recognizing the text on number plates.

We will be using the EasyOCR library to perform OCR on the detected number plates. EasyOCR is a high-performance OCR library that is designed to be easy to use. With the EasyOCR library, we will be able to recognize text in multiple languages and get the results in a matter of seconds.

So, let's get to work!

8.1. Number Plate Recognition in Images

We will follow the same process as we did when detecting number plates in the previous part. So we will write the code for the OCR part inside a function that we will call **recognize_number_plates**.

This way we can reuse the function for both images and videos and easily integrate it with the number plate detection code to build a complete system for recognizing the text on number plates.

Let's add the following code inside the **detect_and_recognize.py** script:

```python
# ...
def detect_number_plates(image, model, display=False):
    # ...

def recognize_number_plates(image_or_path, reader,
                            number_plate_list, write_to_csv=False):

    start = time.time()
    # if the image is a path, load the image; otherwise, use the image
```

The output video will be saved in the same directory as the script with the name **output.mp4**. Here is a screenshot from the output video:

Number plate detection on a video

As we can see in this screenshot, the license plates are detected with good accuracy. The number plates that are closer to the camera are more easily detected than those that are further away. There are various factors that influence the detection, such as the brightness, the angle at which the camera is positioned, the quality of the images, etc. All in all, the algorithm does a good job of detecting license plates.

So there you have it, you know now how to train the YOLOv8 model on a custom dataset to detect number plates and how to use it to detect number plates on images and videos.

```
        image = cv2.imread(image_or_path) if isinstance(image_or_path, str)\
                                    else image_or_path



if __name__ == "__main__":
    # ...
```

The **recognize_number_plates** function takes four arguments:

- **image_or_path**: We can pass either the path of the image or the image itself to the function. When we are working with a video, we will pass the frame itself to the function, but when we are processing an image, we will pass the image's path.

- **reader**: The EasyOCR reader object that we will be using to perform OCR on the detected number plates.

- **number_plate_list**: This is the list of number plates that we will be passing to the function. This list is obtained from the **detect_number_plates** function.

- **write_to_csv**: This is a boolean value that indicates whether we want to save the result to a CSV file. We will be using this argument when we are processing an image.

Inside the function, we are checking if the **image_or_path** argument is a path or an image. If it is a path, we will load the image using the **cv2.imread** function. Otherwise, we will use the image itself.

Now, let's loop over the detected number plates and perform OCR on each one of them:

```
    for i, box in enumerate(number_plate_list):
        # crop the number plate region
        np_image = image[box[0][1]:box[0][3], box[0][0]:box[0][2]]

        # detect the text from the license plate using the EasyOCR reader
        detection = reader.readtext(np_image, paragraph=True)

        if len(detection) == 0:
            # if no text is detected, set the `text` variable to an empty
string
            text = ""
        else:
            # set the `text` variable to the detected text
            text = str(detection[0][1])
```

```
                    # update the `number_plate_list` list, adding the detected text
        number_plate_list[i].append(text)
```

Let's take a moment to understand what we are doing here. We are looping over the list of number plates and for each one of them, we are cropping the region of interest (ROI) using the coordinates of the bounding box.

Notice the **paragraph=True** argument in the **readtext** function. This argument tells the function to automatically combine the detected text.

Without this argument, the output of the function will be a list of items, where each item is a tuple containing the coordinates of the bounding box of the detected text, the detected text, and the confidence score.

An example is better than a thousand words, so here is an example of the output of the **readtext** function without the **paragraph=True** argument for the following image:

Output:

```
[([[7, 22], [82, 22], [82, 60], [7, 60]], 'IN5 9', 0.906076173443513),
 ([[68, 12], [209, 12], [209, 68], [68, 68]], 'Aq1515', 0.6493721724590543)]
```

As you can see, the text from the number plate is detected into 2 parts and each part has its own confidence score and bounding box coordinates. By using the **paragraph=True** argument, the function will combine all detected text into a single string. This is basically what we want here because we want to update the **number_plate_list** list with the whole text of the number plate.

Here is what is the output of the **readtext** function with the **paragraph=True** argument:

```
[[[[7, 12], [209, 12], [209, 68], [7, 68]], 'IN5 9 Aq1515']]
```

After that, we are checking if the list returned by the **reader.readtext** function is empty, which means that no text was detected. If it is empty, we set the text to an empty string. Otherwise, we set the text to the detected text.

Finally, we are updating the **number_plate_list** list, adding the detected text. Here is what will look like the **number_plate_list** list after updating it:

```
[[[91, 302, 206, 338], 'KLI3 AA 8340'], [[488, 304, 528, 327], '']]
```

So as you can see, the **number_plate_list** list now contains the coordinates of the bounding box *and* the detected text.

The last thing we need to do in our function is to check if the **write_to_csv** argument is set to True. If it is, we will save the result to a CSV file:

```python
if write_to_csv:
    # open the CSV file
    csv_file = open("number_plates.csv", "w")
    # create a writer object
    csv_writer = csv.writer(csv_file)
    # write the header
    csv_writer.writerow(["image_path", "box", "text"])

    # loop over the `number_plate_list` list
    for box, text in number_plate_list:
        # write the image path, bounding box coordinates,
        # and detected text to the CSV file
        csv_writer.writerow([image_or_path, box, text])
    # close the CSV file
    csv_file.close()

end = time.time()
# show the time it took to recognize the number plates
print(f"Time to recognize the number plates: {(end - start) * 1000:.0f}
```

```
milliseconds")

    return number_plate_list
```

Basically here, we are opening the CSV file, creating a writer object, and writing the header. Then, we are looping over the **number_plate_list** list and writing the image path, bounding box coordinates, and detected text to the CSV file. Finally, we are closing the CSV file.

At this point, we have everything we need to recognize the text on number plates. Let's integrate the **recognize_number_plates** function in the code for image and video processing:

```python
if __name__ == "__main__":

    # ...

    # Check the file extension
    if file_extension in ['.jpg', '.jpeg', '.png']:
        print("Processing the image...")

        image = cv2.imread(file_path)
        number_plate_list = detect_number_plates(image, model,
                                                 display=True)

        cv2.imshow('Image', image)
        cv2.waitKey(0)

        # if there are any number plates detected, recognize them
        if number_plate_list != []:
            number_plate_list = recognize_number_plates(file_path, reader,
                                                        number_plate_list,
                                                        write_to_csv=True)

            for box, text in number_plate_list:
                cv2.putText(image, text, (box[0], box[3] + 15),
                            cv2.FONT_HERSHEY_SIMPLEX, 0.5, COLOR, 2)
            cv2.imshow('Image', image)
            cv2.waitKey(0)
```

Inside the *if* statement for images, we are calling the **detect_number_plates** function to detect the number plates. Then, we are checking if there are any number plates detected. If there are, we will call the **recognize_number_plates** function to recognize the text on the number plates.

Finally, we are looping over the **number_plate_list** and use the bounding box coordinates to draw the detected text below the number plate.

Okay, so let's test our code with some images:

Number plate recognition in images

As we can see, our OCR engine has successfully recognized the text on the number plates.

Let's test our code with other images, this time our model will not work as well:

Number plate recognition in images

The model has made several mistakes. For example, in the top left image, the text is
"TN74AH1413" but the model has detected **"INZ LAHI43"**. In the top right case, the model didn't
detect the text at all from the second vehicle. So, as you can see, the model is not perfect.

As I said before, our goal in this book is to have a working prototype, not a perfect model. If you
want to learn how to improve the accuracy of the EasyOCR model, you can check out this
article: Improving the quality of the output.

8.2. Number Plate Recognition in Videos

Let's now test our OCR engine with videos: We have our **recognize_number_plates** function
ready, so all we need to do is to integrate it in the code for video:

```
if __name__ == "__main__":
```

```
    # ...

    elif file_extension in ['.mp4', '.mkv', '.avi', '.wmv', '.mov']:
        # ...

        # loop over the frames
        while True:
            # ...

            number_plate_list = detect_number_plates(frame, model)

            if number_plate_list != []:
                number_plate_list = recognize_number_plates(frame, reader,
                                                            number_plate_list)

                for box, text in number_plate_list:
                    cv2.putText(frame, text, (box[0], box[3] + 15),
                                cv2.FONT_HERSHEY_SIMPLEX, 0.75, COLOR, 2)

            # end time to compute the fps
            end = time.time()
            # calculate the frame per second and draw it on the frame
            fps = f"FPS: {1 / (end - start):.2f}"
            cv2.putText(frame, fps, (50, 50),
                        cv2.FONT_HERSHEY_SIMPLEX, 2, (0, 0, 255), 8)

            # ...
```

So we did the same thing as we did for images. After detecting the number plates (using the **detect_number_plates** function), we are calling the **recognize_number_plates** function to recognize the text on the number plates.

Then, we simply loop over the **number_plate_list** and use the bounding box coordinates to draw the detected text below the number plate.

Let's test our code with a video:

Number plate recognition in videos

When you test the code with videos, you will notice that when vehicles are close to the camera, the text on the number plate is generally detected more accurately than when the vehicles are far away from the camera.

Furthermore, you might face some other issues when using the system on videos: Jittering and Fluctuation of OCR output.

Jittering refers to the small, rapid changes in the position of the number plate in consecutive frames which is caused by the movement of the vehicle. The jittering can cause the bounding box around the number plate to become unstable, making it difficult to accurately recognize the text.

Fluctuation of OCR output, on the other hand, is when the OCR engine gives inconsistent results for the same number plate in different frames. This can be due to factors such as lighting conditions, the angle of the number plate, the quality of the image, etc.

To address these issues, you can try to improve the quality of the image by using image pre-processing techniques such as histogram equalization, contrast adjustment, blurring, thresholding, etc. You can also use object tracking algorithms to track the number plate in consecutive frames (for example, 10 frames) and then get all the bounding boxes of the same ids in these frames, use OCR on all the bounding boxes with the same id, and keep the OCR result that repeats the most.

We will not cover these techniques here as they are out of the scope of this book. However, if you are interested in learning more about them, I recommend you check out my articles on image processing with OpenCV and learn more about how to implement object-tracking algorithms.

9. Create a Web Application with Streamlit

9.1. Introduction

In this chapter, we will cover how to use Streamlit to create a web application that will allow us to upload an image of a vehicle and get the recognized number plate as the output.

Streamlit is a powerful open-source library that makes it easy to create and deploy web-based applications with little to no knowledge of HTML, CSS, or JavaScript.

9.2. Installing Streamlit

Before we start building our web application, we need to install Streamlit. Streamlit can be installed using the pip command. Simply run the following command in your terminal and you are good to go:

```
$ pip install streamlit
```

9.3. Creating a New Streamlit App

With Streamlit installed, we can now create a new Streamlit app. To do this, we will create a new directory (**web_app**) and then create a new Python file inside it. We will name our Python file **app.py**.

Here is how our project structure will look like:

```
├── datasets
├── detect_and_recognize.py
├── number-plate.yaml
├── preprocessing.py
├── runs
├── training.ipynb
└── web_app              # new directory
    ├── app.py
    └── uploads
```

Now we will import the Streamlit library inside the **app.py** script and create a basic Streamlit app:

```python
import streamlit as st

st.set_page_config(page_title="Auto NPR", page_icon=":car:", layout="wide")

st.title('Automatic Number Plate Recognition System :car:')
st.markdown("---")



st.markdown("<br><hr><center>Made with ♡ by "
            "<a href='https://dontrepeatyourself.org"
            "'><strong>DontRepeatYourself</strong></center><hr>",
            unsafe_allow_html=True)
```

We can now test our app by running the following command in the terminal (make sure you are inside the **web_app** directory before running the command):

```
$ cd web_app
$ streamlit run app.py

  You can now view your Streamlit app in your browser.


  Local URL: http://localhost:8501
  Network URL: http://192.168.1.7:8501
```

Open the URL in your browser and you should see the app running:

Basic Streamlit app

9.4. Adding Upload Feature

Next, we will add the feature to upload an image. We can use the **st.file_uploader** function to achieve this. This function returns the uploaded file, which we can then use to perform the number plate detection using our YOLOv8 model.

Let's add this feature to our app:

```python
import streamlit as st
from ultralytics import YOLO
from easyocr import Reader
import cv2
import os
import sys
sys.path.append(
    os.path.dirname(os.path.dirname(os.path.abspath(__file__))))
from detect_and_recognize import detect_number_plates,
recognize_number_plates


st.set_page_config(page_title="Auto NPR", page_icon=":car:", layout="wide")
```

```
st.title('Automatic Number Plate Recognition System :car:')
st.markdown("---")

uploaded_file = st.file_uploader("Upload an Image 🚀", type=["png","jpg",
"jpeg"])
upload_path = "uploads"

if uploaded_file is not None:
    pass
else:
    st.info("Please upload an image to get started.")

st.markdown("<br><hr><center>Made with 🤍 by "
            "<a href='https://dontrepeatyourself.org"
            "'><strong>DontRepeatYourself</strong></center><hr>",
            unsafe_allow_html=True)
```

First, we are importing all the required libraries and packages used in our number plate recognition system.

We are also importing the **detect_number_plates** and **recognize_number_plates** functions from the **detect_and_recognize.py** script. But before that, notice that we are adding the parent directory of the **web_app** directory to the system path. This is because the **detect_and_recognize.py** script is located in the parent directory of the **web_app** directory. If we don't add the parent directory to the system path, Python will not be able to find the **detect_and_recognize.py** script.

As I said before, the **st.file_uploader** function returns the uploaded file:

```
UploadedFile(id=2, name='aa2b3501-31.jpg', type='image/jpeg', size=32652)
```

So we can check if the uploaded file is not **None**. If it is not **None**, we will perform the number plate detection using our YOLOv8 model. If it is **None**, we will display a message to the user to upload an image.

Let's test our app after adding the upload feature:

Automatic Number Plate Recognition System 🚗

Upload an image ✔

Drag and drop file here
Limit 200MB per file • PNG, JPG, JPEG

Browse files

Please upload an image to get started.

Made with 💜 by DontRepeatYourself

Streamlit app with upload feature

9.5. Integrating our Number Plate Recognition System with Streamlit

Okay, so now we have our basic Streamlit app with the upload feature. So the next step is to integrate our number plate recognition system with the web app. We will use the **detect_number_plates** and **recognize_number_plates** functions to perform the number plate detection/recognition.

Let's write the code to perform the number plate detection/recognition:

```python
# ...

if uploaded_file is not None:
    # construct the path to the uploaded image
    # and then save it in the `uploads` folder
    image_path = os.path.sep.join([upload_path, uploaded_file.name])
    with open(image_path,"wb") as f:
        f.write((uploaded_file).getbuffer())
    with st.spinner("In progress ...🛠"):
        # load the model from the local directory
        model = YOLO("../runs/detect/train/weights/best.pt")
        # initialize the EasyOCR reader
```

```
    reader = Reader(['en'], gpu=True)


    # convert the image from BGR to RGB
    image = cv2.cvtColor(cv2.imread(image_path), cv2.COLOR_BGR2RGB)
    # make a copy of the image to draw on it
    image_copy = image.copy()
    # split the page into two columns
    col1, col2 = st.columns(2)
    # display the original image in the first column
    with col1:
        st.subheader("Original Image")
        st.image(image)

# ...
```

So, when an image is uploaded by the user, we will save it in the **uploads** folder. We will then load the YOLOv8 model from the local directory and initialize the EasyOCR reader. We will then convert the image from BGR to RGB (because OpenCV reads images in BGR format) and make a copy of the image to draw on it.

Next, we are using the **st.columns** function to split the page into two columns. We will display the original image in the first column and the image with the detected number plates in the second column.

Now, we will call the **detect_number_plates** function to detect the number plates in the image and pass the result to the **recognize_number_plates** function to recognize the number plates:

```
    number_plate_list = detect_number_plates(image, model)

    if number_plate_list != []:
        number_plate_list = recognize_number_plates(image_path, reader,
                                                    number_plate_list)

        for box, text in number_plate_list:
            cropped_number_plate = image_copy[box[1]:box[3],
                                              box[0]:box[2]]

            cv2.rectangle(image, (box[0], box[1]),
                          (box[2], box[3]), (0, 255, 0), 2)
            cv2.putText(image, text, (box[0], box[3] + 15),
                        cv2.FONT_HERSHEY_SIMPLEX, 0.5, (0, 255, 0), 2)
```

```
            # display the number plate detection in the second column
        with col2:
            st.subheader("Number Plate Detection")
            st.image(image)


        st.subheader("Cropped Number Plate")
        st.image(cropped_number_plate, width=300)
        st.success("Number plate text: **{}**".format(text))

    else:
        st.error("No number plate detected.")


# ...
```

As we did before, we will call the **detect_number_plates** function to detect the number plates in the image. If the **detect_number_plates** function returns an empty list, it means that no number plate was detected. In this case, we display an error message to the user. Otherwise, we call the **recognize_number_plates** function to recognize the number plates.

We then loop over the number plates detected and draw a rectangle and the text of the number plate.

Finally, we display the image with the detected number plates in the second column, and below the 2 columns we display the cropped number plate and the text of the number plate.

Let's take a look at the final result:

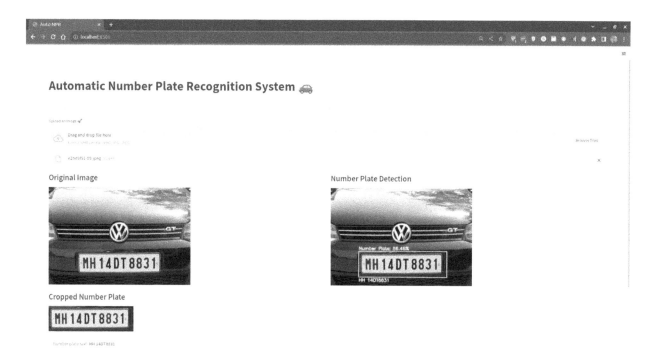

Number plate recognition web application

As you can see in the image above, the original image is displayed on the left and the image with the detected number plates is displayed on the right. The cropped number plate and the text of the number plate are displayed below the image.

Our number plate recognition system is working perfectly. Let's test with another image where the number plate is not detected:

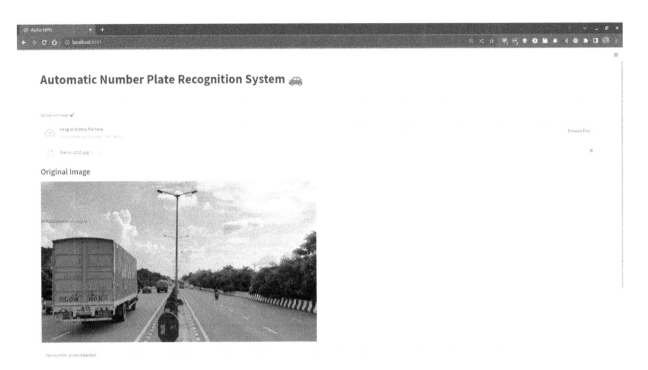

Number plate recognition web application. Here the number plate is not detected by the YOLO model.

When no number plate is detected, an error message is displayed to the user as shown in the image above.

10. Conclusion

Congratulations on making it this far 🎉. You have just taken a huge step in learning about object detection, the YOLOv8 model, OCR with EasyOCR, and number plate recognition.

Let's take a moment to recap what we have done and learned in this book:

- You learned about object detection and deep learning-based object detection algorithms.
- We went through the environment setup process and installed all the necessary packages, including CUDA and cuDNN.
- We discussed the importance of data preparation, including gathering and labeling the data with the help of Label Studio.
- We trained the YOLOv8 model on our labeled data and tested it on images and videos.
- We learned how to apply OCR using the EasyOCR package to recognize the text from the number plates.
- Finally, we built a simple web application with Streamlit to showcase the number plate recognition system.

Our YOLOv8 achieved a pretty good accuracy of about 90% (when the number plate is not too small or too far away from the camera). For the recognition part, we used EasyOCR, which provided a good balance between accuracy and speed. It worked flawlessly and gave us satisfying results.

To take things a step further, the ideal method for license plate recognition would be to use a tracker along with the OCR system. This way, you can track the best OCR result from frame to frame, delivering even better and more stable results.

With all the knowledge and experience you have gained, you are now equipped to take on your own projects and continue to expand your skills. I hope this book has provided you with a strong foundation and sparked a passion for computer vision and AI. Keep exploring and creating! You've got this.

If you have any questions, suggestions, or feedback, feel free to contact me on Twitter, LinkedIn, or via email at cinorouizi@gmail.com. I would love to hear from you.

Happy coding ⚫

www.ingramcontent.com/pod-product-compliance
Lightning Source LLC
Chambersburg PA
CBHW080544060326
40690CB00022B/5219